Being an exceptional wife
An ultimate guide to protecting your husband

Vicky Bright

Table of content

Introduction

Women with attributes of a good wife are deserving keepers, and they deserve all the care and respect since they have the purest intentions for the family.

One of the reasons why a woman is dubbed an exceptional wife is because of her willingness to make the marriage succeed. When the pair disputes, an excellent woman would follow the example of her husband and be amenable to resolving matters peacefully.

Also, an exceptional woman recognizes her husband cannot be flawless, therefore she does not attempt to shape him into her ideal image. Rather, she conforms to his nature and corrects his faults when he errs.

Being an excellent wife does not only need being a wonderful wife but also requires being able to preserve and defend the spouse God has given you.

(pro 20:6 Most men will declare each his own virtue, But who can discover a loyal man? The upright man lives in his honesty; His offspring are blessed after him). It is tough to find a nice and trustworthy spouse who will remain true to you, it is thus our obligation as a woman to protect them so that they can be a joy to our family.

An excellent wife demonstrates attributes that not only assist construct a house and family but also helps her present herself as a decent human being. It is crucial to know what to do to protect your spouse and marriage as a whole.

Chapter 1

Pray for your husband
Fervent prayer is highly powerful
Praying for your husband is one of the most vital things you can do for the health of your marriage. Calling on God to bless your husband will not simply help him; it will affect your entire family for the better.

Whether your partner is aggravating you or not you must pray for him. Rather than confronting him on everything he does or doesn't do, take your requests to the Father–the one who can genuinely influence your husband.

And don't simply petition God for the things you wish changed in your husband. Pray for his requirements. Pray for his day. Pray for his spiritual growth and strength. The biggest method you can support your husband is to cease bothering him, trust in God's work in his life, and pray for him daily.

There is a contrast between letting God operate in your husband's life and confronting your husband when he is genuinely doing something wrong. Choose your battles and be iron that sharpens iron, not nails on a chalkboard.

There are various strategies to cover your husband in prayer. Here are some vital prayers to pump your husband up as you go through life together.

- Pray for his abilities to lead spiritually.

Your husband is supposed to be the spiritual leader of your home. The book of Ephesians states, "The husband gives leadership to his wife the way Christ does to his church..." (5:23 MSG). If your husband is already a wonderful spiritual leader, pray for him to improve in faith and to remain true over the years.

Many men are not qualified to lead their families spiritually. If you realize that you and your husband are in this circumstance, pray for him to get stronger over time. Ask for doors to be opened in his life that will bring him closer to God. In the interim, live a virtuous life and treat your husband with respect, "so that even if some [husbands] do not hear the word, they may be won without a word by the conduct of their wives" (1 Peter 3:1 ESV)

- Pray for his prayer life.

Your husband's relationship with God is important to his growth as a spiritual leader–and, in fact, his success in all parts of life. Pray genuinely that he will faithfully reach out to God in prayer in good times and in bad. Encourage him to spend time alone with God, but also to lead your family in prayer.

- Pray for your marriage.

Keeping God first in your marriage is important to its success. Pray that your husband will follow God's demands of him, and pray that you will also be a godly wife to your husband. Ask that the two of you will come out of horrible circumstances stronger and closer than ever and that no internal or external factors will be allowed to divide you. "Because God fashioned this biological union of the two sexes, no one should disrespect his art by tearing them apart" (Matthew 19:6 MSG)

- Pray for his strength of character.

J.C. Watts famously stated, "Character is doing the right thing when nobody's looking." The quality of your husband's character will either positively or unfavorably impact every part of your life. Pray for him to assess his behaviors and his effect on others through the lens of his character. Pray that he would continuously seek to self-improve.

You'll see him at his finest and his worst—and often, you'll be the only one who sees how he behaves when no one else is looking. Always encourage him to make the proper choices, even when it's most hardest. Use your specific influence as his wife to help him be the best version of himself, and pray for your ability to help him safeguard his character.

- Pray for his bond with your children.

If you have children, ask God to help your husband develop a deep, loving bond with them. Pray for his ability to lead others by example. Pray that he will be able to level with them and comprehend the world through their eyes as he makes daily decisions about guidance and discipline. If your husband is striving to break undesirable patterns inherited from his family of origin, pray specifically for him to be able to overcome them.

- Pray over your sex life.

It may seem like a strange proposition, but praying for your sex life to improve is a terrific way to bless your partner (and you will be blessed, as well. God is thrilled when you are entirely connected. Involving Him in the most intimate aspect of your life will assist the two of you to connect fully to the spiritual level that God wishes for husbands and wives to experience. You can never go wrong with asking God to bless your lovemaking!

- Pray for him to be at peace amid hardships.

When terrible circumstances occur, be ready with the prayer that, no matter what may happen, God will pour His peace over your husband, as well as your family. In the book of Philippians, we're counseled on precisely how to plead for peace: "[D]o not be concerned about anything, but in everything through prayer and supplication with thanksgiving let your requests be made known to God. And the peace of God, which surpasses all understanding, will preserve your hearts and your minds in Christ Jesus" (4:6-7 ESV)

Turmoil, misery, and stress may swiftly strip a marriage of its closeness, a family of its connection, and a person of his or her soul. Pray that your husband will be able to continue through the inevitable storms, and pray that he will infuse God's peace in you and your children as he leads you.

- Pray for a fruitful professional career.

These days, many men (and women!) find themselves battling in their work. They're confronted with job shortages, economic challenges, and a variety of other hurdles. Perhaps your husband has taken a job just to get by–maybe it's not in his area of ability, or maybe it's with a less-than-stellar organization. He might be moving forward every day despite being unsatisfied with his profession.

Support him and pray for him in his present circumstances, but also hope that he will be able to shift into a profession that is gratifying and rewarding. Pray that he will be able to utilize his God-given abilities to make a livelihood for your family and that he will be blessed with a profession he's enthusiastic about.

- Pray for his safety and good health.

It's a no-brainer: your husband's health and safety are highly vital. Cover your husband in prayer daily as he goes about his business, asking God to protect him in every capacity. Who better to approach for protection that the Lord himself? He is the ultimate guardian.

- Pray for his objectives to be achieved.

Whether or not you know all your husband's objectives and desires, pray that God will bless and fulfill the ones that are in accord with His purpose for your family. Supporting your husband's objectives, both in prayer and via your connection with him, will thrill and motivate him.

Your support, or lack thereof, will make or destroy him. Combine your supportive presence with intense prayer in his favor, and watch him flourish.

protect your husband from criticism and attacks from you and your family

Everyone hates to be criticized. Yet, for some reason, couples frequently feel permitted to disparage, berate, harass, and blame one other in ways they'd never do with friends. Criticism in married relationships is so widespread that makes the cliche "intimacy fosters contempt" unshakably rock solid. Why do couples revert to critical conduct while knowing deep down it is destructive and damaging to their relationship?

What precisely is criticism?

Couples frequently have a tough time discerning between criticism and expressing a complaint. Criticism may have severe repercussions since it makes the recipient feel abused, rejected, and harmed. Couples believe that if they agree to avoid criticizing they won't be able to have a talk about broken commitments or pledges.

For example, if your husband dumps his clothing and towels on the floor instead of putting them in the hamper. If you criticize the husband by stating, You are lazy or You never clean-up after yourself' that is criticism. If instead you say, I would really appreciate it if you would put your clothing in the hamper, it is expressing a complaint.

Criticism is an assault on your husband's character. Calling your husband lazy or pointing out a negative personality defect is criticism since you are condemning your husband as a full person. In contrast, if you express a complaint, and concentrate on a particular action or conduct, and call for a different action or behavior, it is distinct from criticism.

Why do partners act as though criticism in married partnerships is okay?

The closer we are to a person, the more we see their flaws and weaknesses. Over time we get annoyed, our patience wears thin, and our self-restraint weakens. For example, we may find our friend endearing, but if he were our husband, no doubt his forgetfulness would have inconvenienced or even hurt us over time, and we would be tempted to lie to him about it.

With friends, acquaintances, colleagues, and others we can usually keep our negative reactions and criticism in check. We don't see them every day, can take a break until our irritation wears off, or their behavior doesn't affect us personally. But those with criticism in marriage relationships often don't afford their partner comparable restraint and respect. Criticism becomes their default habit even if deep down they know it isn't right.

Why is criticism in married partnerships so common?

One may assume that the last person we'd want to harm would be your marital husband, the one you love. Intimacy frequently can generate disdain, but why do women choose to concentrate on bad qualities instead of the great parts of their husband. Why doesn't closeness beget appreciation instead?

It appears that our brains are equipped with a built-in "negative bias". Our brain is geared to instinctively put greater weight on bad news or unpleasantness. Negative bias comes in naturally at the initial stages of processing information. As a consequence, our attitudes are more significantly impacted by depressing news than uplifting ones. Is it any surprise therefore that frequent criticism by a wife shifts the balance of a relationship from routine to miserable?
ignored, criticism in married partnerships destroys the fabric of the relationship. Unhealthy criticism undercuts the primary

pillars of effective relationships: safety, acceptance, and approval. Regular criticism steals the vibrancy and spontaneity from a partnership.

"How can a husband tolerate continual criticism in a married relationship?

Husbands adapt to a wife continual criticism by utilizing numerous survival methods, such as Self-protection

He dashes for cover. To survive psychically, he retreats inside a cocoon of self-protection. Some develop an exceedingly protective demeanor to insulate themselves from the sharp whip of the judgmental wife. Others suppress their "authentic selves" as a protection mechanism, letting forth just the portion labeled "partner approved". They may feel the need to reduce their individuality to prevent disparagement which might end in loss of self.

-Distancing.
To fight off criticism in a married partnership, a husband surrounds himself with a secure buffer zone from which he answers respectfully as if from afar. Friends, job, children, exercise, social media, television, literature, and newspapers may function as buffers.
-Withdrawal

A criticized husband withdraws and becomes emotionally unavailable. He protects the "self" by erecting a wall to keep the critical wife away. He refuses to interact or respond when criticized. Instead, he accepts it and most likely builds another brick in the wall of anger each time they are insulted, belittled, or berated. Things are a rare individual who can let it go every time.

-Substance Abuse

Another typical response to criticism in a married relationship is hias well as a variety of other major issues.

Most of what we know about relationships we learnt unintentionally from our families at a very early age. If we had a critical parent, we may be critical too or partnered with a critical person, or both. We presumably adopt the survival methods outlined above. Unfortunately, duplicating our early background and taught patterns generally do not create joyful healthy partnerships. We need to extend our horizons and study more.

The good news: human beings are intellectual and flexible. With knowledge and understanding, we can alter and adapt.

Chapter 3

Don't act on a negative advice

In many parts of life, we have family members and friends willing to give us unwanted advice.

At times this advice is based on extensive experience, experiences, tribulations, and sometimes even credentials. However, there are situations when the advice is plain awful wrong.

What follows is a compendium of terrible relationship advice that will most likely lead you to an age of relationship misery and disagreements.

While individuals who provide this advice may have good intentions, we recommend you remain away from these whoppers. When in question about the direction of your marriage or troubles within it, seek expert assistance.

Friends and family members may either make or unmake your marriage by the sort of counsel they provide to you.
Don't allow your relatives and friends to teach you how to behave in your relationship.

Your friends in no way have the authority to control your relationship or make any choices for you or your husband. Neither should you be the type of buddy that gives out needless advice and makes choices for any of your buddies.

If you want to achieve a lot in your marriage, or life, you frequently have to push yourself to do things you've never done before. This can imply accepting a promotion that is a stretch. Taking a job in a new sector. Making a career transition. In many circumstances, your ability to come up to speed fast relies on seeking guidance. Lots of guidance.

But not all counsel is made equal. Some advice is just awful. And discerning excellent counsel from poor advice isn't always straightforward. Bad advice may sound nice. Good counsel might make us uncomfortable which can cause us to disregard it. Use these questions to help you figure out whether the advice you are getting is worth listening to.

Does this individual have an ulterior motive? Not everyone has your best interest in mind. Sometimes it's simple to detect when someone has something to be gained in a manner that drives them to provide inappropriate counsel (or, more commonly, "constructive feedback" that is damaging). A buddy who may be cautious of your husband may warn that being governed by your husband "won't assist you." But other times it's less evident. Ask yourself whether this individual has anything, even something very little like their own sense of themselves, to be lost or gained by your success in marriage. This is a reason why receiving counsel from a broad circle is so crucial. Bad advice may also be well-meaning — a parent who believes your marriage will drag you down, for example. But the closer someone is to you, either emotionally or professionally, the less objective they may be.

Is this person a professional? Lots of individuals have opinions. Some individuals are experts. Seek out, professionals. What makes someone an expert? As the Dunning-Kruger effect has proved, the less someone learns about a topic, the more certain they are in their view. So concentrate on experiences – how the individual whose counsel you are seeking came to achieve their expertise. Seek counsel from others who have done what you are attempting to achieve, preferably many times. When an expert provides you with advice, give it serious thought. If someone is merely expressing an opinion, consider it again.

Have I heard this advice from others? The greatest protection against poor advice is obtaining lots of advice from lots of specialists. You will rapidly see trends and similarities. That will ground fresh advice for you by enabling you to compare it to what you've heard previously. A good counsel will be verified, often several times. This inquiry is also the strongest protection against disregarding excellent advice that you simply don't like. At some point, if you hear something frequently enough you need to think that it could be meaningful. You still don't have to like or even follow it but you should be cautious not to reject it out of hand.

Chapter 4

Understand that other women love your husband and are capable of anything

In any relationship, there's always someone ready to distract either of the husbands. It might be at their place of work, online, or a random individual in a random situation. It occurs to both men and wives in a marriage.

There's always a circumstance of a lady flirting with another's husband. You may be experiencing the same thing in your relationship. Whether it appears trivial or big enough to damage your relationship, it's something to tackle in no time. It's common to have confused thoughts about how to respond to a scenario like this.

But, paying attention to your attitude at a key moment like this should be your top goal. It may seem too difficult if you think about it, but it's not impossible.

Men are different than women, particularly sexually. Men are activated visually and physically. They are physiologically driven - on a time cycle set early in life.

Men often have a higher sexual urge than women, at least in the early years of marriage. Men typically battle with temptation to dirty ideas more often than women. The single greatest thing you can do to defend your husband from other women is to keep your own fire blazing at home. Take care of yourself – at least try. Take time to be romantic, particularly during the day, (go ahead and contact him at his workplace and say something surprising!)

Good sexual expression needs time and planning. (Some of you will never have genuinely pleasurable sex until you calm down - you're just too frantic.) Take a snooze. Get the youngsters to bed early. Arrange for a motel date. Take time to listen to your hubby. Learn to look him in the eye. Flirt with him. Buy a stunning nighty. Learn to relax. Learn to like yourself; develop confidence.

Learn what gives him pleasure and thrills him. Admire his physique. Get a little foolish occasionally. Do something insane. Initiate things once in a while. Find out how he wants you to dress for him and then execute it.

When the fire's blazing at home, he's less likely to be warming his hands someplace else. Get interested in this topic before it's too late. Someone out there deems your husband handsome. They'd want to have him for their own. Fight back! Protect him, by working at your relationship. A marriage is a dreadful thing to squander.

Chapter 5

Protect him from the pressure of the household

Ladies, it's YOUR obligation to make your relationship an inviting one. You have to welcome your husband, as he is, with open arms. It's your obligation to send him out knowing things are taken care of at home and giving him a place of comfort–a safe haven–to return to at night.

Are you supporting your husband with your actions and your words? Or do you bring him tension and tear him down? Does your husband know what to anticipate from you or does he dread getting home because he never knows what he will get?

Is your house (and your heart) a warm, serene, and welcoming place for him to return to each day?

If you are treating your husband in a manner that makes him feel at ease in your house, you are going to pull him out and make him a better man!

While marriage may be a great and gratifying experience, no permanent relationship is likely to function smoothly at all times.Life may be full of ups and downs which can occasionally stress the strength of your marriage.

Some factors put tension and strain in a marriage and this includes

1. Finances
Finances may very quickly become a cause of tension and concern within your marriage. In challenging economic situations husbands might have to worry about topics such as jobs, mortgages, bills, raising children, healthcare. The accompanying stress and strain might affect your husband and as a consequence, the

relationship can be under pressure. It is crucial to be able to discuss financial concerns with him in a helpful and constructive manner in order to be able to handle them in the best possible way.

2. Children

Having children may be one of the most amazing experiences in life although motherhood can also put a burden on a marriage.

Deciding when to have children may be tough for couples. One of you may not feel ready to commit to having children early in your marriage or may wish to wait until a later stage for a number of reasons including professional opportunities.

The birth and upbringing of children might also stress you out at times. Parenthood comes with it a shift in lifestyle. In addition to the pleasures of having a kid, motherhood may bring sleepless nights, and anxieties about feeding and maintaining a newborn which can all be a shock to the system for couples.

Fertility troubles may be quite distressing for couples seeking to have children. This may be a very tough scenario for couples to find themselves in. Some couples suffer miscarriages which may be highly terrible events. Parents may also lose a kid which is every parent's dread.

3. Work Commitments

Whether your husband is highly career-focused working full or part-time his profession might demand a lot from him. Work might eat up time that he would want to spend with you and the children. Pressures at work may affect him and he might find himself angry or agitated by the time he reaches home.

His employment may also need him to spend periods of time away from home and this may be quite tough for you the wife. In such instances, you might have a significant sensation of loneliness. This may be especially challenging for you since you will have to handle all the tension and strain from the children

4. Difficult Behaviors

It is possible that you and your husband may go through a tough moment at some point in his life together. Whether it's the consequence of relationship challenges, job-related concerns, family difficulties, or personal trauma, these stressful situations may often contribute to folks being difficult to get along with.

Husbands who have been reasonably easy to get along with might become distant, despondent, angry, defensive, argumentative, or secretive when under strain and this will surely influence their relationship.

Stress may also result in your husband being engaged in habits that can become detrimental over time. Drinking, self-medicating, and gambling are just examples of activities that may grow out of hand and make issues much worse.

It is preferred that you recognize and speak about any behavior that is becoming troublesome and help your husband to attempt to fix them.

In order to reduce these pressure that affect most marriages there should be

-Effective Communication
Communication (talking and listening) is vital to good relationships and marriages. Open, honest, and respectful

communication can assist you to cope with the hardships and tribulations you endure in the course of your life together. Without a healthy pattern of communication, wives may become unconscious of and inattentive to their husband's ideas, wants, and emotions. Lack of communication may result in couples lacking comprehension of each other, becoming insensitive towards one another, and growing estranged from one another.

Ensure you make time to communicate with your husband every day. The more you listen and converse with one another, the closer you may get. The closer you are, the simpler it is to communicate, share and collaborate to solve difficulties that emerge.

-Being Attentive

Pay attention to your hubby. Notice stuff about him. Has your hubby been silent, aloof, busy, or less communicative lately? Does he look anxious or under pressure? Is he spending a lot of time at work, or is he feeling emotional a lot of the time?

Although the following may not be grounds for great worry, they may occasionally be signals of problems that a person is feeling and finding difficult to disclose.

If you sense that your husband is upset or frightened, make time to chat with him and tell him that you are there to listen and support him.

This will assist him to recognize that you are eager to help in any manner you can.

-Spending Time Together

Spending time together is a crucial aspect of preserving and strengthening your marriage. It may assist you to appreciate one another, enjo.by another's company, have fun, increase your knowledge of one another, communicate more, connect with one another, and reduce stress. The quantity of time you offer to someone is a sign of the value you place on them.

By spending as much time as you can together, you may stay linked emotionally, physically, intellectually, and spiritually and this connection can develop as time goes on.

Chapter 6

Be his best friend

What comes to mind when you think of the traits you appreciate in your closest friend? They're probably easy to be around. You could spend all day in each other's presence and yet want to continue with the talk.

They know everything about you, good and bad, yet are never judgemental. You know they've got your back, and you have theirs. You may call each other anytime, day or night. If required, you know you would drop everything to be by each other's side.

Now, does this describe your relationship with your husband?
marriage, we frequently characterize the connection as "the finest friendship with sex included!"

When we speak about being best friends with someone, what are some of the things that spring to mind? Here are some ways individuals describe their best buddies. These may sound like what your marriage once entailed but possibly no longer do.

-They understand me without having to explain anything.
-They bring out my greatest traits – my intellect, curiosity, willingness to investigate problems, sensitivity, service to others, humorous side, and more.
-When I'm sad, they help me recall my excellent characteristics.
-They never judge me.
-They allow me to have poor days/moods and recognize they have nothing to do with them.
-They allow me to feel depressed but don't let me remain there too long.
-They know my favorites: meals, music, hobbies, and dress style and are usually on target with birthday gifts.
-Know all my past and love me despite the blunders I've done.

-Can hang with me all day and never get bored, even if we don't speak anything.
Feel satisfaction in my triumphs and are never envious of my wind

Being your husband's closest friend means you have to be there for him in good times and bad. When your partner is feeling sad or depressed, indicate that you care about their state of mind. Don't shrug off their feelings with a "cheer up! Things can't be that bad!" Sit down and ask them to tell you what's going on. Nod and indicate that you are hearing them.

"It's reasonable that you'd feel sorry about it" is a fantastic method to demonstrate you actually listen to them. You don't need to provide answers, you simply need to show them you are there.